Dewpoint

Dewpoint

Poems by
Amanda Foulger

Hand to Hand
Topanga, California

Hand to Hand is a community based endeavor that supports independently published works and public events, free of the restrictions that arise from commercial and political concerns. It is a forum for artists who are in dynamic and reciprocal relationship with their communities for the sake of peacemaking, restoring culture and the planet. For further information regarding Hand to Hand please write to us at: P.O. Box 186, Topanga, CA, 90290, USA. Or visit us on the web at:

www.handtohandpublishing.com

Printed in the United States of America

Book and Cover Design by
Stephan David Hewitt

ISBN 978-0-9720718-3-3

First Edition 05 04 03 02

This book is set in Plantin and printed on acid-free, recycled paper using soy-based inks.

For Life

with gratitude to my Spirits, Teachers and Ancestors

CONTENTS

Dewpoint

Canyons and Passes

Scoured by winter winds,
what's loose, flies off,
what's brittle, breaks.

Home my shelter,
but no protection,
no matter my resistance
to these intermittent wails,
rough limbs, tattered wishes,
sharp leaves' insistent
scratching on my walls.

Even lined with skins
and blankets, windows rattle,
doorways leak, no shield against
chilled nights of restless sleep.

Hunched and tired, one simple morning,
I sit, hands warmed by sunrise tea.
Dissolution rudely whistles
its fierce entrance into my frail house.
Surrendering, I finally see
there's no returning
to the fiction of who I used to be.

Vision Quest - Canyonlands, Utah

In the blue cave of my retreat,
all my beloveds are here: those I called
and those who heard my song of reconciliation.
Wind wakes the hair on my body, blows through my bones.
Water washes the stones of my old stories.
Tall red cliffs stand sentinel.

In the sacred grove of cottonwood, juniper and pine,
the trees instruct me on the second day:
the three sisters, the two couples – one growing apart,
    one coming together.
A single tree stands strong in the center.
Rocks and sun heal and ground me.
Mineraled earth slows me down.
The stream sings a chorus of our essential happiness.
On a rock at water's edge, bright grasshopper greets me.
Curious lizard becomes my bold and watchful companion.
Coyotes talk and hunt close by near dawn.

On the third day, I sit in a gully facing east
among stones tumbled from steep surrounding palisades,
heaved up from fire and water to slowly crumble
down through centuries of rain and sun.
Two I find: a black heart rock banded by a perfect white circle,
a reminder of the immense cliff-side heart in last night's dream,
and my own heart's awakening that brought me here.
A coiled stone snake I hold to help me shed my skin.

The fourth day, sky calls and I look straight up to see
long clouds exhaled over deep blue space.
There I am, body fully extended, flying south over the mesas.

The word "striving" comes, but there's no strain. I'm simply
    going for it.
My hands reach forward, come together, and grasp the future.
I see myself and another come together affectionately.
It's me and myself meeting, here in Mother's Heart.

The last warm night of new moon vigil,
winds gust through hours of lightning and thunder,
flashing and echoing across the great plateau,
above, below and all around our sacred canyon.
Clouds slowly cover the immense star field above the trees.
Lightning sparks the land that rises to meet it in holy embrace.
The blessed rain finally falls. Life is renewed.
My quest is done and sealed with spattered kisses.

Hawk's Song

Do not fear.
I sing the sun up,
soar high above,
see earth revolve in light's embrace.
See you.
Your whole life has led you
to this present breath
now dawning.
This gold is yours.
Eat it and sing.

Moon

I'm having dinner with the Moon.
She's smiling at me,
conversant in so many languages
she understands my heart.
Mottled pearl in an indigo sky,
tonight she tells me something of hers:
beneficent sister circling us.

Bathed in mutual luminosity,
we're sweet family,
basking in the great night sky
together.

Where I Live

At the year-round stream below my house
old ones ground acorns in stone bowls.
They still notice who comes and goes,
who sees them there in shadows and stones,
faint traces left in sand.

Beyond the bank, a tiger lily blooms
for no one in particular, bright curls
on a waving stalk. You'd miss it
if you weren't looking beyond debris
washed down from winter rains.
Its late exuberance signals spring
has nearly bled into summer.
The stream too runs slower, lower now
to falls below the mountain,
mingling waters in the canyon bottom creek,
meandering to the sea.

I too may linger or run out.
Or simply rise up
blooming when it's time
to leave this place.

Casa de Dom Ignacio

"No one is forgotten," She tells me,
delicate bare feet moving over the Casa grounds.
Blue robe flecked with stars,
She bends and embraces each in perfect time.

Senhor and the Saints stride over long red hills
and through the current rooms, called by prayers,
anchored by years of the Medium's devoted service.
Ignacio's burning dedication,
the Doctors' skilled and healing hands,
the Spirits' vast compassion
pour over us like the emerald green water
bubbling from cleft rocks below
into stream, waterfall and pool,
miraculously singing life's renewal.

Wash. Wash yourself here.
Go out onto the *plana* barefoot,
and offer what you have.
Drink deep and remember colored parrots clustered in spare
flowering trees and the small wild bees making honey.
Graceful black and white-winged tic birds sound
and dance on dry earth in the flame gold sunset
while heavy brahmas roam the fields.
Beneath the ground, a multitude of crystals grow
in brilliant rainbow veins of light.
Here we mine our treasures.
Here we come to love.

August 2002
With heartfelt thanks to medium and healer John of God, Heather
and all at the Casa in Brazil.

13

Visitor

White cat sits like a Sphinx
in the palm of a three-branched oak,
finally revealed after weeks
of flashed appearances
in a neighbor's bedroom,
food scattered in another's kitchen,
yaps of nervous dogs.
I'd heard its evening getaways in grass
glimpsed pale shadows under trees,
knew some strange creature was around.

Now we meet,
do a slow trespaso,
eye to eye.
It gives nothing,
belongs to no one,
lives no one place.
Reminds me
I'm a visitor too.

Coyote Mind

Tawny Coyote, shawl marks across her shoulders,
waits to cross the stream of cars to hunt
for gophers, cats, leftovers and unsuspecting birds.
Infinitely adaptable, she doesn't mind
the wait. Meals are served on many tables.
Mountain prey are sung to their deaths;
here, stealth and cleverness is how they go.
At dawn, she dreams of hunting on the Milky Way,
coughs up stars to feed her young.

Bête Noir

Walking my bête noir,
It breaks loose; I run in hot pursuit.
It laughs, and I'm undone by its wild cleverness,
leading me on, then dashing away,
digging holes and howling in my sculptured landscape.
Barking taunts, out of reach,
it pauses; I approach.
Teeth bared, ears back,
mouth slavering, it's ready to kill.
I grab, it darts into the trees.

Realizing I need help, I call the karma police.
A Goddess arrives, astride a tiger,
magnificently attired in red and gold,
bejeweled and crowned in regal authority.
I can't believe Her many arms,
the weapons She carries with such ease.
I tell Her my bête noir is running loose
tearing things up, making trouble.
She coolly sees my agitation, fear and pain,
invites me to her temple.

Exhausted and ashamed,
but oh so grateful,
I arrive with flowers, late, I think,
but find the ritual has just begun.
Relieved, I lay myself and fresh picked flowers at Her feet.
"Take me, take my madness, loss and hurt.
I'm here and I surrender!"
Shining bowls of food and water are sung and offered,
    whisked away.

At peace, with gratitude, I finally rest. The puja ends.

On my way out, amazingly I get a message:
my bête noir will meet me for lunch.
He tells me how unhappy he's been,
how tight the collar, short the chain,
his power unused, needs neglected.
No shitting in the wild, no running nose to savage earth,
no pleasure of fresh meat, or rolling in old feces and dead fur.
My love renews for my dark beast.
And in his eyes, I see my self-absorption, foolish pride,
the box I kept him in.
He's whole, and home,
not lost, but found and free.

Spring Moon

Come my darling,
we don't want to miss the great moon
rising over the mountain;
above it, a star connected by a thread.

Come, my dear
we can just catch it.
Let's open the wine and ride as far as we can
through this sapphire sky
celebrating together.

If we're ready,
we'll go where life begins again.
There, mountain lilacs scent the air,
lilies reach through hollow stems
in adoration of the light.
Leaves unfurl in shimmering symmetry.

This is Spring's promise:
to reveal the truth of who you are,
and in the budding branches,
who you've always wanted to be.

Forgetting

A hollow silence in my chest:
again, my heart has forgotten where it is.
When distracted,
it sometimes skips a beat,
then hurries to catch up.

So close,
this side,
and that;
drum's rhythm
may fall there,
instead of here,
if I don't pay attention.

It asks:
Which side are you on, anyway?
Then I remember where I am,
the work at hand,
this life I am living.

Animal Dreams

Teeth circled by easy lips,
not bared now,
but sharpened on bones,
ready to bite
if you come too close
or I get hungry.

Long grooved nails
on padded paws, dig, catch and cut.
Solid shoulders, thick strong neck,
connect to heavy jaw as I doze in sunlight,
feel what moves, smell
what breathes around me.

Perched high on a rocky edge,
my eyes pierce the landscape.
The wind lifts; I lean into it effortlessly,
circle wide, scan for flesh to feed our fragile young.
One focused mind.

Fall Browsing

Walking a wet morning meadow
of faded grass and mounded vines,
the last wild brambleberries offer themselves.
I taste: some sour, some sweet, some turned fermented wine.

Angled sun strikes trembling red and amber leaves
that punctuate deep greens at forest's edge.
Old Cedar brushes reassuringly as I enter
the silent grove. Bright moss encircles
its heart. Rich earth well worked by gophers
sprouts spare weeds both tough and sweet.

Leaving the trees, there's a web
strung tight across my way.
It pulls on me as I pass through,
along with thoughts of you.

I cross the sluggish stream,
step onto the road to see
a sign edging the property:
No Hunting and No Trespassing,
a message for you.
Flicking my white tail, I leap the boundary
on delicate hooves
re-enter my sanctuary home.

The Gift

For M. W.

On a nearby mountain, fossiled shells,
swirled stones remain from
earth's volcanic thrusts and gushes.
Walking there, a friend gifts me
a four-bloomed branch of mountain poppies.
Three, still gorgeous, are on their graceful way
through fading, wilting, dying.

Suddenly I know with certainty
that three quarters of my life is past,
its last quarter like the final blossom:
soft white petals blown open,
around a fringed heart,
high sun yellow
burning brightly at its center.

Spring

Spring has come and with it, you, compelling and ardent.
I'm alone in this northern valley,
yet these woods too are ripe with us.
Bumblebee grasps open blossom, nuzzles deep.
Amorous red salamanders cavort in a mossy pool.
Cedar's tender fingers beckon from embracing limbs.
Sap eagerly ascends, pours out white hawthorn, purple lilac.
Wild blue lilies rise through fresh deer tracks
on my moist earth.
On a new forest path I'm entranced by the faint perfume
of a pastel rhododendron.
In this morning sweetness I hear your voice,
imagine soon your kiss.

Taoist Poem

All we need is here for our perfect realization.
Sinned against and sinner sit side by side,
neither lost and both forgiven.
Those graced and those whose graces are all used up:
mirrored sides of the same lake in which we swim.

However made, our nets of circumstance are holy.
Let go.
Don't stiffen or cling.
Become one with the water,
and you'll pass right through.

For Friends Recently Come Through Illness, Myself Included

Now that you have saved your life
– this time – live it!
Make poems of the dead spiders in the bath,
bodies wrested from our common ancestors.

Swimming in this sea of words,
which story will I tell?
The life lived
or the one unknown
which can only arise
from this perfect moment?

Now I remember You in a medicine dream,
familiar Beloved,
your form elusive, face hidden.
You said it was You
who would be in everyone and everything I loved.
Right now, I haven't forgotten.
But forgive me when I do,
wasting time looking for You.

House-Sitting

For D. & M.

Sleep slowly rises from my flesh
as I stand on this hill,
watching reflected sunlight
glide across the western mountain.

An early wind subsides and abundant life is everywhere.
Three plump quail forage in the garden patio
on their royal walkabout.
Miffed, the jay squawks in a nearby tree.
Rabbit carefully investigates the perimeter, listening,
while the wisteria embraces the eaves.

Now the earth has turned
and the risen sun shines behind me.
I marvel at the inner translucence
of the gold glass Kwan Yin on the sill;
I'm still working on mine.

Thank God for the generosity of these openhearted friends
who support life in its multitudinous forms.
Through their own devotions they have arrived here
and keep on arriving.

Mother Pine

Summer's pine bleeds gold:
luminous drops distilled
from wounds and water,
ground and growth.
Liquid from the cutting edge of life.

Her roots mine earth's moist density,
extracts its essence,
draws it up her trunk.
Angled arms become stiff fingers
to read the changing winds.

Worked by weather, light and night
she offers pollen to her people,
then fruit of tight green cones.
They revolve and open slowly,
cast her seeds of medicine to earth.

Birthing done, pine sighs,
sweat dries and with laments
and rustling lullabies,
exhales thick honey down her sides.

Dark and Light

This eclipse, a wild card
on the full moon's round:
light edged with shadows
of what remains unlived,
all we might have been,
what's done and what's to come.

Cool light blinks, reflects clearly
what is here, and all the possibilities,
dark and bright, within and around us.
The truth of what change will demand
from us outlined like the rabbit
silhouetted on the nighttime hill,
its shape and movement clear,
but no features or dimension.

All of us turning on the fulcrum
of our one and only life
this night. Stars etched
in a silent but watchful sky,
wonder which way
we'll go in the morning.

Otherness

An itch began one day above my breast,
persisted like a droning bee near open flowers,
sometimes close, then far-away.
It bloomed into a small pink spot:
an insect's nip or allergy, I thought.
Ointments soothed, but it persisted.

Then I remembered a summer day
I clipped and cleaned my garden;
the green remains in my embrace.
A sharp thin limb that poked
a farewell to my chest
as I pushed cuttings into compost.

The otherness of plant
insisting to be remembered.
Branch to bone, bark calling skin,
hair and leaves entwined,
my mammal's breath exchanging
with its final respiration.
Its cells converting sunlight into form.
Me consuming seed, leaf, tuber,
fruit and nut – my body made of otherness.
The sap from that tree
kept knocking on my heart
till I knew it for my blood.

Out Of My Mind
For C. V.

I lost my mind while sitting by the river.
A rock called me to see a leaping swordfish on its side.
A tree became a standing serpent diving into blue.
Another was a sentry owl.

I walked beside the long stream of time.
Ancestral voices whispered tales, sang bittersweet.
Old ribbed buffalo now set in stone invited me to ride.
I found secrets stippled under bark.

Illuminated by a bright imprint of our First Sun, I stood in awe.

Tenderly blanketed by a light gray mist,
later,
I found my way home.

Homecoming

While I was away, the plum leafed out,
sheltering young fruit.
Below, tasseled grasses reach up
to touch this new green life
even as their stalks and nodding pods
tan brittle brown and faded gold
in mounting heat and light.
In me too, life and death
converge this summer season.

Weed

This roadside weed
grows in crazy circles,
a standout in the crowd.
Dizzied, likely overwhelmed
by fumes and countless drive-bys,
maybe twisted by its attempts to speak
in metal, plastic, oil's exhaust.
Certainly intelligent, it makes me wonder
if it's been twirling with night galaxies.
I look again: it trembles in response.
Now it's teaching me to dance.

Tai Chi

For my teacher, R.H.

Picking celestial morning fruit
on an island park in a busy city
I turn and am astonished to see
a great blue heron perched
high on a large topped pine.
Koi swim in cool waters beside us.
One now sleeps in his belly.
The hunter rests and digests,
undisturbed by traffic
or the harsh alarms of flyby crows.
He tucks one leg beneath his body,
folds his sinuous neck to meditate.
We begin the Form; I turn,
grasp bird's tail to the right
and he is gone.
Sage's gift, this visitation.

Tao Mountain

All this living on borrowed,
bought or stolen water
makes me uneasy.

How has it become so difficult
for us to sit beside our ancient streams,
half submerged this thirsty winter,
watch water dragons play?
Fins flash, scales shine,
water shimmers
in flickering sun and shade.
They won't survive, removed
too many times and miles from home.

Born from cloud sky nurseries,
these elemental beings
fall as rain, fill our springs,
refresh us all with primal water,
enough for just this place,
the ten thousand things existing here
and nothing more.

Eldering

Here's my tooth.
Take it and chew me well.
Swift, clean bites.
No lingering.

My sight? All right.
Clouds slowly coalesce now
behind even the necessary lenses
and there's no remedy.
Just help me see what matters.

Sore muscles, tendons tight
from seasonal digging in rocky ground.
Increasing work to crest the hill, hold the thought.
Brain by cell by bone,
you consume me piecemeal.

My heart you leave till last, the tastiest bite.
Don't be surprised if I fight.
You'll finally love me to death, of course,
but you'll never have my light.

Dust

For D.C.

Absent just a few days,
yet when I return
dust greets me:
a fragile constituency
risen from some other place,
or fallen mysteriously from above.

Airy particles and bits have coalesced,
adhere to feet of chairs, collect in hollows,
feather shelves, float across my floor.
An invisibility so hungry or curious
it mates with dirt, seeps under doors,
embraces spider webs, coats surfaces
of leaves and window panes,
peoples my home with pale wisps
and shadows blown here from nothing.
It wants life's wanting.

Was this what gathered earth
from space, this longing?
The invisible desiring form,
cohering into touch,
imagination's breath made tangible.

The two must long for one another,
bound by some mysterious attraction.
Fire's love for wood
transforms it into ash and smoke;
tree's last embrace becoming emptiness.

All this back and forth:
our bodies visiting
between our endlessness.
You and me,
our touch like lightning,
sparks igniting
the true dimensions
of our conversation
till love's knowledge
releases us again
to dust.

Winter Bath

Slipping stiffly into the morning comfort
of warm water, steamy aromatic air,
my cold body drinks in the moisture
and the heat. I slowly turn and melt.

The icy dark one at last releases me
from its deadly grip, lifts off and away.
Ancient beak clacking,
its dry thick-skinned wings
beat shadows over these mountains,
as it fades into the distant day
to visit rage, doubt, darkness,
loss and insufficiencies
elsewhere.

Thankful, I stand,
dripping sweet water,
freed of winter's curses,
my skin rosy,
heart cleansed and new.

Shaman's Heart

Glass sparkles on dark pavement as I drive home,
jeweled stars thrown down from the Big Bang
by an unwitting drunk in mourning,
or cocky kids hunting for love or trouble.

Grieving our lost relatives
or looking for the next best party,
we've forgotten our family is already here
and the party's nearly done.
Time to clean up and get ready for the new day.

Dewpoint

Blessed trees, sweet grasses,
in forests, fields, dear friends,
you enact the mystery
of our daily condensation
from the Source,
sweet giveaway to all.

Dewpoint, holy breath of transubstantiation:
the moment of exchange when water
you've breathed up to the skies
returns to earth again refined in drops,
purest nectar, creation's child.
This sacred elixir, your bodies' blood,
refreshes, heals, inspires, joins what's divided,
makes life whole. Your selfless work
becomes our daily grace and blessing.

Day and night, fire and water,
those ageless lovers also meet in us.
Our cyclic respiration a part of
earth's miracle of creative circulation.
Each one of us a crucible,
each breath an alchemy,
each life a personal distillation
of who we are, whatever we have learned:
our gifts, these words, our prayers,
our offerings back to Life.

Acknowledgements

Heartfelt thanks to the fine poets and writers in my life for their particular inspirations, excellence, encouragement and friendship:

Deena Metzger – poet, writer, teacher and healer, co-founder of Hand to Hand for her dedication to creativity, healing and beauty.
Doraine Poretz – poet, teacher, playwright for her devotion to her calling, her generosity, gifts and passion.
Beth Buerkens – poet, shamanic practitioner and teacher for her support and heart in both worlds.
Mary Jane Evans – writer and teacher, for her insights, talents, encouragement and sensibility.
Maia and Marsha de la O – poets and writers for their brilliance, craft and beauty.
The late poet Anne Silver for her humor, grit, energy and love, who invited me into the poetry community.

Gratitude to family and friends – in particular:

My sister Rachel, life-long bedrock of support for me and my work.
My son Ram for coming home to himself.
Heart family Michael Park, Dan Jordinelli.
Medicine sisters Susan Lynch, Corey Hitchcock.
Artists Nancy Mozur, Angie Bray & Steve DeWitt.
My late, great cousin James Ingebretsen – now a muse.
Stephan Hewitt – co-founder of Hand to Hand whose astrological insights, editorial and production skills made this book possible.

The poem "Hawk's Song" has appeared in The Foundation for Shamanic Studies' *The Shamanism Annual* and in the *Shamanic Visions* 2010 Calendar by Amber Lotus.

Amanda Foulger *is a full-time Shamanic Practitioner based in Topanga, California. She has trained with The Foundation for Shamanic Studies (FSS) since 1988 in core shamanism and has a broad background in spiritual study and practice for over thirty years. She teaches for FSS in the greater Los Angeles area, in Santa Barbara and Colorado, as well as assisting at their Advanced Shamanism and Shamanic Healing programs on the West Coast.*

She has a private practice in shamanic counseling, training and healing services. Amanda also teaches her own theme-based shamanic workshops under the general title of Our Personal Medicine, and, as a minister, conducts personal and group ceremonies and rites of passage. She can be contacted at:

P. O. Box 557, Topanga, CA 90290
afoulger@aol.com